Financial Survival

Personal and Financial Organization

by Ray H. Weinrub, C.L.U.

Third Edition

ASPEN WEST

FINANCIAL SURVIVAL: Personal and Financial Organization

Written by: Ray H. Weinrub, C.L.U.
Cover Illustrated by: Ernie Harker

Copyright © 1990; 2nd Edition, 1994; 3rd Edition, 1995;
    Ray H. Weinrub

ISBN# 0-9615390-8-9 Paper Back
ISBN# 1-885348-18-5 Three Ring

Aspen West Publishing Company, Inc.
8385 Sandy Parkway, Suite 129
Sandy, Utah 84070
(801) 565-1370

PRINTED IN THE UNITED STATES OF AMERICA

Note: **This handbook is intended as a workbook only. You should seek licensed legal counsel in the state where you reside for any legal advice. Aspen West Publishing Company, Inc., assumes no liability regarding the legal construction of the documents in this handbook.**

God asks no man whether
he will accept life.
That is not the choice!
You must take it.
The only choice is how.

–Henry Ward Beecher

Dedication

To my wife, Shirley, who is responsible for this entire endeavor.

Acknowledgements

I would like to thank the following, without whose help this handbook would not have been possible: Guy Wong, CPA; Morgan Johnson, attorney at law; Harriette Abels; Marlene Chernev; Mel Chernev; and Harriette Schwartz.

Table of Contents

Part V: Priorities

<u>Appendices</u>

Foreword

Thirty-five years in estate and financial planning have taught me an important fact: in most cases when a spouse dies, *the surivor desperately needs help.* Chaos sets in quickly.

Most of that chaos occurs because the survivor simply doesn't know where to begin. There are taxes, mortgages, and other bills to pay; investments to manage; and urgent decisions to be made. The survivor needs to know all sources of income, where important documents are located, and how bank accounts are accessed. Too often, that information is scattered—or not available at all. Why? Because most people avoid talking about death. Others decide the whole estate situation is simply too complicated, so they avoid it altogether.

That's why this handbook was created. You can use it right now—whether you're planning for the future or faced with the recent death of your spouse. It's a personal guide—filled in by *you* with your own information—that will give you peace of mind and financial security in the event of your spouse's death.

–Ray H. Weinrub, C.L.U.

Introduction:
Why You Need This Handbook

Until now, no one has published a clear, concise, easy-to-use handbook that puts everything you need to know about surviving a death at your fingertips.

Until now, that is.

What you hold in your hands is a one-of-a-kind handbook that provides the details you'll need to turn chaos into order. Best of all, it's customized: because *you* fill in the blanks, it's a unique record of what *you* need to know and do.

Regardless of your situation, you need this book. Maybe you're young; the information you gather will start you on the road to intelligent financial organization and planning. Maybe you and your spouse are both young and healthy; this handbook will save you thousands of dollars by helping you organize your own information–without attorneys and tax advisors. Maybe you've never been married; you still need the kind of organization you'll learn in this handbook.

If you're facing your spouse's death–or that death has already occurred–the information on these pages will help you quickly establish order and avoid costly mistakes.

So pick up a pencil–*now*. Start filling in the information–*now*. Maybe it's tough to talk about–or think about–but it will be much tougher if you wait until a tragedy occurs. If you're married, go through the exercise with your spouse; it's critical that *both* partners know the information it lists.

Some of the information will be easy to fill in–your attorney's name and address, the name of your auto insurance company, the type of pets you own. Some of it will be more time-consuming or complicated: researching a stock portfolio, gathering up documents, determining how you want to dispose of your property. If you've never done so before, you might have to learn some new terms–401K, 1099, preferred stocks, defined benefits. **Just remember this: whatever time and effort you invest now will save you tremendous time, effort, confusion, and heartache in the future.**

A few final notes of advice:

Fill in this handbook thoroughly, even if you normally keep your records on computer (or have a tax advisor who does so). This handbook provides you *instant* access to the information you'll need, even in the event of power failures, hard disk corruption, or simple inability to operate a software program.

Keep the filled-in handbook in a safe place, but *do not put it in a safe deposit box until you verify that the box will not be sealed upon a death.* Notify two close family members or heirs about the handbook, and tell them where it can be found.

Finally, remember to review and update the handbook periodically. You'll find blank pages throughout that will make it easy for you to make notes, comments, updates, and changes.

Okay. Grab a pencil. If your spouse has just died, skip to Part III and follow the guidelines for things that need to be done immediately; come back later and fill in the rest. If you're still in the planning stages, turn to Part I. **Go!**

Part I

Getting Started

Chapter 1
Getting Started

Getting started is generally the hardest part of any project–but the tips listed here will help you get going right away!

First, make a list of the professionals you may need to call on for help. Include people like your physician, attorney, accountant, and insurance agents. Get addresses and phone numbers. You'll need this list as you fill out the pages in Chapter 16.

Next, make a list of your expenses. If you and a spouse each contribute to the monthly bills, make sure you compare notes. If you're paying on loans or mortgages, write down the account numbers and financial institutions you pay. Note whether bills are due monthly, quarterly, semi-annually, or annually. You'll need this information when you figure out your net worth in Chapter 5–and your cash flow in Chapter 8.

While you're at it, make a list of the things you own and how much they are worth. Make sure you include the basics–your home, your furniture, your personal property, your cars, cash on hand, and any money you have in checking or savings accounts–as well as your more exotic assets, such as coin collections, country club memberships, and stocks and bonds. This information will round out the picture of your net worth in Chapter 5.

If you own a business, you'll need to gather additional information and note it on one of the blank pages in this handbook. Make a list of everything you'd need to know to run the business. Ask the accountant, chief financial officer, or comptroller for help.

Finally, sort through your financial paperwork. It's time to throw away what you don't need and organize what you do. Basically, you should keep all income tax returns *forever*. Keep receipts for all tax-related bills you've paid for five years (even though the statute of limitations for substantiating your records is three years). If you don't know what kinds of receipts to keep, get a copy of last year's tax forms; the categories will help you organize.

You should also keep:

- Paperwork regarding home improvement projects
- Receipts for large purchases (such as appliances or furniture)
- Records showing that promissory notes, contracts, loans, and deeds have been paid
- Receipts, bills, canceled checks, and records newer than five years old

How are you going to organize what you've gathered? That's strictly up to you–and to the volume of paperwork you have. You might try a three-ring binder, a sturdy box with a lid, a set of expandable file folders, or a filing cabinet. Whatever you choose, label things clearly so you can find them easily.

Now that you have your paperwork organized, you can start filling in this handbook. Begin on the next page!

Chapter 2
Personal Information and
Where It's Found

Date these records were updated_____

Male name_____
Birthdate_____
Mother's maiden name_____
Social Security number_____
Driver's license number_____
Military number_____
Where discharge papers are located_____
Passport number_____
Where passport is located_____
Employer_____

Female name_____
Birthdate_____
Mother's maiden name_____
Social Security number_____
Driver's license number_____
Military number_____
Where discharge papers are located_____
Passport number_____
Where passport is located_____
Employer_____

NOTES, CHANGES, AND UPDATES

Date of marriage_____

Where marriage certificate is located_____

Cemetery name_____

Cemetery address_____

Plot number(s)_____

Religious affiliation_____

Funeral director_____

Address_____

Vehicle year and make_____

Where title/pink slip is located_____

Vehicle year and make_____

Where title/pink slip is located_____

Bank (checking)_____

Address_____

Checking account number_____

Where checkbook is located_____

Bank (savings)_____

Address_____

Savings account number_____

Where passbook is located_____

Bank (Cds)_____

Address_____

CD account number_____

Term_____ Interest rate_____

Where passbook is located_____

Safe deposit box location_____

Where keys are located_____

NOTES, CHANGES, AND UPDATES

Credit union_____

Address_____

Account number_____

Where papers or passbook are located_____

Club Memberships (Golf, Tennis, etc.)

Name_____ Card number_____

Address_____

Name_____ Card number_____

Address_____

Copyrights, patents_____

Where trademark papers are located_____

Coin collection value_____

Where the collection is located_____

Make a note on the opposite page regarding what you want done with the coin collection when you die.

Stamp collection value_____

Where the collection is located_____

Make a note on the opposite page regarding what you want done with the stamp collection when you die.

Credit card_____

Account number_____

Emergency phone number_____

Credit card_____

Account number_____

Emergency phone number_____

NOTES, CHANGES, AND UPDATES

Credit card_____

Account number_____

Emergency phone number_____

Credit card_____

Account number_____

Emergency phone number_____

Gasoline credit card_____

Account number_____

Emergency phone number_____

Department store credit card_____

Account number_____

Department store credit card_____

Account number_____

Deed_____

Where the deed is located_____

Deed_____

Where the deed is located_____

Deferred compensation plan_____

Organization_____

401K investment plan_____

Company contribution_____ Your contribution_____

IRA account number/name_____

Address_____

Type_____ Annual contribution_____

Where records are located_____

NOTES, CHANGES, AND UPDATES

Keogh account number/name_____

Address_____

Type_____ Annual contribution_____

Where records are located_____

Other Pension and Retirement Plans

Name_____

Type_____

Where records are located_____

If you need additional space, please use the opposite page.

Joint venture agreements_____

Where records are located_____

Please note specifics on the opposite page.

Limited or other partnerships_____

Certificate number_____

Number of shares_____ @ _____Total price_____

Where certificate is located_____

Broker_____ Firm_____

Phone number_____

If you need additional space, please use the opposite page.

Mortgages and real estate_____

Address_____

Deed name_____

Mortgage policy number_____ Premium_____

Where mortgage policies are located_____

Where previous home papers are located_____

_____

NOTES, CHANGES, AND UPDATES

Lease agreements_____

_____

Where lease agreements are located_____

Notes payable_____
To whom_____
Address_____
Due date_____ Interest_____
Period_____
Where records are located_____

Notes receivable_____
From whom_____
Address_____
Due date_____ Interest_____
Period_____
Where records are located_____

Securities and Investments
Company_____
Certificate number_____
Purchase date_____
Type: • Common
               • Preferred
               • Bonds
               • Debenture
               • Mutual fund
               • Money market
               • Municipal bond
*If you hold multiple securities and investments, make a separate
sheet on each one and attach the sheets to this section.*

NOTES, CHANGES, AND UPDATES

Trusts
Family revocable number_____
Registration date_____
Children's trusts_____
Living trusts_____
Testamentary trusts_____
Where trust papers are located_____

Income Tax Records
Where current records are located_____
Where previous years' records are located_____
_____
_____

Will
Where will is located_____
Date of most recent revision_____
Date codicil added_____
Attorney_____
Address_____

Miscellaneous Financial Papers
Where salary check stubs are located_____
Where commission statements are located_____
Where other income statements are located_____
_____

If you need additional space, please use the opposite page.

Alarm company_____
Permit number_____
Address_____
Phone_____
Special instructions_____

NOTES, CHANGES, AND UPDATES

Where instruction booklets are located for the following:

Refrigerator_____
Stove_____
Microwave oven_____
Washer and dryer_____
TV and VCR_____
Computers_____
Air conditioning and heating_____
Landscape items_____
Carpet and wallpaper_____
Furniture_____
Where service contracts are located_____

Pet_____
Name_____
Veterinarian_____
Address_____
When shots are due_____

If you need additional space, please use the opposite page.

NOTES, CHANGES, AND UPDATES

Chapter 3
Key Information

Life Insurance

Company_____

Policy number_____

Address_____

Agent_____ Phone_____

Type_____ Face amount_____

Premium amount_____ Due date_____

Owner_____ Beneficiary_____

Loan_____

Riders_____

Company_____

Policy number_____

Address_____

Agent_____ Phone_____

Type_____ Face amount_____

Premium amount_____ Due date_____

Owner_____ Beneficiary_____

Loan_____

Riders_____

Annuities

Company_____ Policy number_____

Address_____

Agent_____ Phone_____

Type_____ Original amount_____

Owner_____ Beneficiary_____

Interest rate_____ How long?_____

NOTES, CHANGES, AND UPDATES

Health Insurance

Company_____ Policy number_____

Address_____

Agent_____ Phone _____

Type_____ Deductible_____

Premium amount_____ Due date_____

Coverage description_____

_____

Company_____ Policy number_____

Address_____

Agent_____ Phone _____

Type_____ Deductible_____

Premium amount_____ Due date_____

Coverage description_____

_____

Auto Insurance

Vehicle_____

Company_____ Policy number_____

Address_____

Agent_____ Phone_____

Premium amount_____ Due date_____

Personal liability and property damage_____

Collision deductible_____

Comprehensive_____ Deductible_____

Medical_____ Towing and labor_____

Rental_____ Umbrella_____

NOTES, CHANGES, AND UPDATES

Vehicle_____

Company_____ Policy number_____

Address_____

Agent_____ Phone_____

Premium amount_____ Due date_____

Personal liability and property damage_____

Collision deductible_____

Comprehensive_____ Deductible_____

Medical_____ Towing and labor_____

Rental_____ Umbrella_____

Homeowner's Insurance

Company_____ Policy number_____

Address_____

Premium amount_____ Due date_____

Type_____ Deductible_____

Personal liability and property damage_____

Use loss_____ Medical_____

Flood_____ Earthquake_____

Workman's compensation_____

Value of personal property in the home:

Jewelry_____ Cameras_____

Art_____ Guns_____

Stamps _____ Coins_____

Sports equipment_____ Other_____

NOTES, CHANGES, AND UPDATES

Vacation Home Insurance

Company_____ Policy number_____

Address_____

Premium amount_____ Due date_____

Type_____ Deductible_____

Personal liability and property damage_____

Use loss_____ Medical_____

Flood_____ Earthquake_____

Workman's compensation_____

Value of personal property in the vacation home:

Jewelry_____ Cameras_____

Art_____ Guns_____

Stamps _____ Coins_____

Sports equipment_____ Other_____

Other Insurance

Company_____ Policy number_____

Address_____

Premium amount_____ Due date_____

Type_____ Deductible_____

Personal liability and property damage_____

Use loss_____ Medical_____

Flood_____ Earthquake_____

Workman's compensation_____

NOTES, CHANGES, AND UPDATES

Chapter 4
Fixed and Liquid Assets

All of the property you own is categorized under the term *assets*. *Fixed assets* are property held for the purpose of doing business–buildings, machinery, property, and so on. *Liquid assets* are property that can easily be converted into cash–such as U.S. Savings Bonds, stocks, bonds, or life insurance policies that have cash value.

When you figure out your *net worth*, as you'll do by filling in the worksheets in the next chapter, you begin by listing all your assets–in other words, all the property you own, both fixed and liquid. You total their value. Next, you list your *liabilities*–t h e debts you owe. Your net worth is what's left when you subtract your liabilities from your assets.

Why is it so important to keep records on your assets? Because you need the information for tax purposes. **The entire area of taxation on assets and liabilities is extremely complicated; consult a tax advisor or attorney to determine your tax bracket and responsibility.**

One of the most important things you can do to protect yourself is to *keep good records*. This handbook is a beginning; filling in the worksheets gives you a good start. And, while you should consult a tax professional for help, the most important records you should keep are those relating to real estate–what you paid, the amount of closing costs, how much you spent on improvements, and how much you sold it for.

*I*t's essential that you keep records on every home you buy and sell. Why? Consider this: if you sell one home and buy a new one for less money, you'll be taxed on the difference. You'll also be taxed if you buy your next home more than twenty-four months after the sale of your previous home.

If your new home costs more than your previous one, and you buy it within twenty-four months, you can defer any tax liability. *K*eeping track of how much you pay for the new home, any closing costs, and how much you spend on improvements can help you "decrease" your profits on the sale, helping you avoid a tax debt.

If you're over the age of fifty-five when you sell and buy, you may qualify for a one-time tax exclusion of $125,000, regardless of whether you have a mortgage balance. To qualify, the home must have been your principal residence for a total of at least three years during the five-year period ending on the date you sell the home.

Here's how it works: assume you bought your home for $60,000; today it is worth $250,000. That's a $190,000 profit. You can prove you put in $20,000 in improvements, which reduces your profit to $170,000. Now deduct the $125,000 exclusion–and you're only taxed on the remaining $45,000.

Remember, **you can only take the $125,000 exclusion once**. It doesn't apply to vacation homes or second homes. If either spouse used the tax exclusion in a previous marriage, it can't be used again in a new marriage. Since you can only use the exclusion once, you should obviously never use only part of it.

There are a number of other issues to consider regarding taxes and real estate; for example, if your spouse dies, you can qualify for what's called stepped-up cost basis, helping you avoid tax liability without using the $125,000 exclusion. These laws are complex, and you should consult a tax professional.

Even a professional can't help you if you haven't kept good records. That's where your part comes in. START TODAY to gather up as much information as you can. Gather receipts, escrow records, and other papers that can help you establish costs. If you don't have these records, do what you can to reconstruct them–contact the business where you bought your carpeting, for example, and ask them for a copy of your receipt.

As you gather up your records, move on to the next chapter–the worksheet will help you determine your net worth.

NOTES, CHANGES, AND UPDATES

Chapter 5
Net Worth Balance Sheet

Date records were updated   _____   _____

Assets (What You Own)

Value of home $_____ $_____

Value of second home $_____ $_____

Other real estate $_____ $_____

Commercial property $_____ $_____

Office equipment $_____ $_____

Business value $_____ $_____

Furnishings/appliances $_____ $_____

Personal property $_____ $_____

Stamp/coin collections $_____ $_____

Club memberships $_____ $_____

Automobiles (Blue Book) $_____ $_____

Limited partnerships $_____ $_____

Joint ventures $_____ $_____

NOTES, CHANGES, AND UPDATES

Art items	$_____	$_____
Cash on hand	$_____	$_____
Money in savings/checking	$_____	$_____
Bank CDs/Treasury bills	$_____	$_____
Credit union accounts	$_____	$_____
Stock/bond portfolio	$_____	$_____
Mutual funds	$_____	$_____
IRA/Keogh accounts	$_____	$_____
Life insurance/annuity	$_____	$_____
U.S. Savings Bonds	$_____	$_____
Pension/profit-sharing	$_____	$_____
Deferred compensation	$_____	$_____
401K investment account	$_____	$_____
Deferred commissions	$_____	$_____
Notes due	$_____	$_____
Other	$_____	$_____
Estimated total	**$_____**	**$_____**

NOTES, CHANGES, AND UPDATES

Date records were updated   _____   _____

Liabilities (What You Owe)

Mortgage on home $_____ $_____

Mortgage on second home $_____ $_____

Mortgage on real estate $_____ $_____

Mortgage on com. prop. $_____ $_____

Insurance policy loans $_____ $_____

Notes/personal loans $_____ $_____

Business liabilities $_____ $_____

Credit card debt $_____ $_____

Auto loan(s) $_____ $_____

Taxes owed $_____ $_____

Other $_____ $_____

Estimated liabilities $_____ $_____

**Estimated net worth
(assets minus liabilities)** $_____ $_____

NOTES, CHANGES, AND UPDATES

Chapter 6
Income

The first step in figuring out a budget and your *cash flow* (how much cash you have to work with each month) is to figure out your total income. Determining a cash flow is a lot like determining a net worth: in a nutshell, you subtract your expenses each month from your income for the month.

Don't stop with your salary–there are plenty of other sources of potential income. Remember income you get from rental property, royalties, alimony or child support, and commissions, for example. The worksheet in Chapter 8 provides a pretty complete list of possible sources of income.

If you haven't been a good record-keeper in the past, **now is the time to start**. As mentioned earlier, it's tough for professionals like tax consultants or attorneys to help you if you can't provide the records. Establish files and start keeping paycheck stubs and other evidence of income.

As you gather and organize your records, keep the following in mind:

• *You need to report all income to the IRS, even if you do not receive a 1099 income statement form from your employer.* If you earn less than $600 in a year from labor or commissions, you may not receive a 1099–**but that does not change your tax liability**.

• If you are married and filing jointly and your modified adjusted income (your income less your deductions) including half your social security income is more than $32,000, *then that half of your social security income is also taxable.* Under President Clinton's new tax laws, the amount of taxable social security income will increase from half to 85 percent.

• If your spouse dies and had an IRA, you can roll over that IRA to yours without paying any taxes. You may also be able to leave your spouse's 401K dollars, annuities, or other plans intact until you need them. Consult your tax professional for details.

• A Family Revocable Living Trust can save you hours of paperwork and frustration in transferring ownership of property when one spouse dies. See Chapter 9 for details. If you don't have this kind of trust, name changes may be required to switch ownership of property, automobiles, investments, tax shelters, and other assets.

• As you figure out your income and establish a budget, **remember to pay yourself first.** If you save money now, you'll have it later!

Should You Become a Landlord?

Many people–especially surviving spouses–are tempted to move to an apartment or condominium and rent out their home. After all, you can almost certainly get much more in rent from your home than you have to pay on an apartment, right?

Probably. But there's much more to consider than that. If you do decide to rent out your home, check out the rental laws in your state. Most are designed to protect the landlord, and you need to make sure you're in compliance. Keep the following in mind as you draft a rental agreement and look for tenants:

> • Specify terms in writing. How much are you charging for rent? Is there a security deposit? How much? What will the tenant have to do to qualify for a refund of the security deposit, if any?

• Specify your cancellation policy. Who can cancel the lease or rental agreement? How much advance notice will you require? Spell out your eviction rules.

• Will you allow pets? What kind? How large?

• Will you allow children? How many? What ages?

• What is the maximum number of people you'll allow to live in the house?

• If repairs are needed, who will pay for them? If you agree to pay, how will you do it? Will you require a written estimate first? Will you ask the tenants to pay, and then reimburse them? If repairs are needed, can the tenants legally withhold their rent until the repairs are made?

• Who will pay for the utilities?

• Will you let the tenants use the garage, carport, yard, and other areas outside the house? Under what conditions?

• Who will be responsible for maintaining the yard? In most areas, the landlord is responsible. Make sure you spell things out in writing.

• What happens if rent payments are late? What will be the penalty? Spell out the specifics in writing.

• Will you have access to the house? Specify your rights in writing.

• Will you allow overnight parking and guests?

• What kinds of restrictions do you want? Will you require no smoking? Be specific.

• *If* you require a cleaning deposit, go through the house before the tenants move in and make a detailed list of all existing stains, scratches, dings, and other damage. Make two copies; sign both and ask that your tenant sign both. At move-out time, you can compare current damages to your original list to determine whether a cleaning deposit should be refunded.

• Will you allow the tenants to sublet (rent your home to someone else)? Under what conditions?

Chapter 7
Expenses

The second part of determining monthly cash flow is to figure out your expenses–the money you need to pay out each month. Most people immediately think of obvious expenses, like rent or mortgage payments, groceries, and utilities. But you need to list *all* your expenses–things like your cable t.v. fee, newspaper or magazine subscriptions, and your life insurance premiums. The worksheet in Chapter 8 provides a good list of possible expenses.

As with income, start by keeping track of the money you spend. There are several ways to do it–you can keep receipts during the month, then total them at the month's end. You can also keep a small notebook in your purse or briefcase, then make a notation *every* time you spend money. **Note: if you do any transactions with cash or with a credit card, don't rely on your checkbook for an accurate total.**

The following expenses bear special mention:

Taxes. Unless your employer withholds taxes from your paycheck, you must pay federal and state taxes quarterly. You are also responsible for making quarterly tax payments on any extra income you receive that doesn't have taxes withheld. You're also responsible for property taxes; if you still have a mortgage, property taxes are generally included as part of the mortgage payment. If you have to pay these yourself, most states ask for half of the payment in December and the other half in April, though due dates vary from one state to another.

Interest. You must pay interest on any money you borrow, including your mortgage; real estate interest is generally included as part of the mortgage payment. Banks and other lending institutions should provide you with statements at year's end detailing how much interest you have paid during the year. Under the new tax laws, you cannot deduct the interest you pay on auto loans, credit cards, or life insurance loans; the new Clinton tax laws may also restrict the amount of interest you can deduct from second homes or vacation homes.

If your home mortgage interest is at 8 percent or higher, you should consider refinancing to reduce the amount of interest you pay. Beginning October 1993, many mortgage companies offered no-cost loans, making it possible to refinance as many times as you want to take advantage of lower interest rates. *However, if you intend to live in your home for more than seven years, it might be wiser to pay some closing costs when you refinance.*

Contributions. Contributions to legal charities or churches are an expense, but also provide a tax deduction; your accountant or tax consultant can provide details. Basically, there are two types of deductible contributions: actual cash contributions and non-cash contributions (such as donations of clothing or furniture to the Salvation Army). *Accurate record-keeping is essential.* Whenever you make contributions, ask for a receipt; if you are making a non-cash contribution, estimate the value of the merchandise you are contributing and have an official from the charity sign the receipt.

Medical expenses. Make sure you keep accurate records of all medical expenses, including doctors, hospitals, labs, dental care, eye care, and health insurance premiums. Remember that you can deduct only a percentage of these from your adjusted income.

Chapter 8
Monthly Cash Flow Worksheet

Date records were updated _____   _____

Income

Husband's salary $_____ $_____

Wife's salary $_____ $_____

Interest income $_____ $_____

Dividends $_____ $_____

Alimony $_____ $_____

Child support $_____ $_____

Note proceeds $_____ $_____

Commissions $_____ $_____

Retirement income $_____ $_____

Social Security income $_____ $_____

IRA/Keogh income $_____ $_____

NOTES, CHANGES, AND UPDATES

Property income	$_____	$_____
Limited partnership	$_____	$_____
Business income	$_____	$_____
Disability income	$_____	$_____
Royalties	$_____	$_____
Trust fund	$_____	$_____
Other income	$_____	$_____
Total monthly income	**$_____**	**$_____**

Make a note on the opposite page of any deductions from your salary for taxes, insurance premiums, retirement, savings, government bonds, union dues, and so on.

Expenses

Rent or mortgage	$_____	$_____
Mortgage insurance	$_____	$_____
Property taxes	$_____	$_____
Mortgage on 2nd home	$_____	$_____
Mort. on vacation home	$_____	$_____
Electricity	$_____	$_____

NOTES, CHANGES, AND UPDATES

Natural gas	$_____	$_____
Water and garbage	$_____	$_____
Telephones	$_____	$_____
Pest control	$_____	$_____
Pool service	$_____	$_____
Landscaping	$_____	$_____
Cable TV service	$_____	$_____
Cleaning	$_____	$_____
Air conditioning/heat	$_____	$_____
Association dues	$_____	$_____
Credit cards	$_____	$_____
Dept. store cards	$_____	$_____
Auto loans	$_____	$_____
Auto license/tax	$_____	$_____
Gasoline/oil	$_____	$_____
Auto repairs	$_____	$_____
Auto insurance	$_____	$_____

NOTES, CHANGES, AND UPDATES

Groceries/staples	$_____	$_____
Clothing	$_____	$_____
Life insurance premiums	$_____	$_____
Medical insurance prem.	$_____	$_____
Accountant fees	$_____	$_____
Legal fees	$_____	$_____
Alimony	$_____	$_____
Child care/support	$_____	$_____
Personal care	$_____	$_____
Education	$_____	$_____
Memberships	$_____	$_____
IRA/Keogh/retirement	$_____	$_____
Gifts/charity	$_____	$_____
Investments	$_____	$_____
Other savings	$_____	$_____
Income taxes/FICA	$_____	$_____
Recreation	$_____	$_____

NOTES, CHANGES, AND UPDATES

Magazines/newspapers	$ _____	$ _____
Notes payable	$ _____	$ _____
Expected travel expenses	$ _____	$ _____
Forced savings	$ _____	$ _____
Miscellaneous	$ _____	$ _____
Total monthly expenses	**$ _____**	**$ _____**

To figure out monthly cash flow, subtract expenditures from income. If you come up with a negative number, *you need to make adjustments.* There are two basic ways to balance out: either increase your income or cut your expenses. Figure out which will work for you, *then go to work to make it work!*

NOTES, CHANGES, AND UPDATES

Part II

Estate Planning Basics

Chapter 9
Wills and Trusts

Regardless of where you are in life, one fact applies: you've worked hard for what you have. With a little planning now, you can guarantee that your family members and loved ones will have the benefit of everything you've worked for. If you fail to plan, your survivors may lose it all. *Even if your estate is very small, your planning can ensure that it passes on to those you designate, not to the state or others.*

This handbook provides a general guide. **You should contact an attorney for all matters related to planning your estate, drawing up a will, or signing legal papers.** Find an attorney who specializes in estate planning; your local bar association can make recommendations. Make sure you understand all fee schedules before you begin any legal work.

Drawing Up a Will

Simply stated, a will is your declaration of what you want done with your property. **Drawing up a will should be your number-one priority**, regardless of your age or the size of your estate. If you die without a will (*intestate*), your property will be disposed of according to the laws in your state–and taxes will probably eat up most of your estate.

You can write your own will–most stationery stores have forms that help you with the basics–as long as you are of "sound mind" (the court is convinced that you knew what you were doing and wanted to do it). After you've drafted your wishes, have an attorney review your will to make sure you comply with all laws and that your heirs will be fully protected. Your attorney can also help your heirs avoid costly tax ramifications. *A good attorney will protect you and make sure that your will stands up legally.*

Once you've written a will, you should review it every two years—more often if your circumstances change dramatically. During this review process, you may decide to draft a *codicil*– a n addition or amendment to a previous will alters, modifies, or explains the original will. Codicils must be written in the same legal language as the original will and must be written while you are of sound mind. You should consider drafting a codicil if any of the following apply:

- The value of your estate changes significantly

- The tax laws change significantly

- Your marital status changes (you marry or become separated, divorced, or widowed)

- The status of your heirs changes due to births, adoptions, marriages, serious illnesses, deaths, or the acquisition or loss of income and property

- You lose affection for an heir and decide to remove him/her from your will

- The person(s) you appointed as executor or trustee dies, moves away, or becomes estranged

- The person(s) who witnessed the signing of your will dies, moves away, or becomes estranged

- You change your mind about charities or other philanthropic interests

You'll need to gather the following information before you actually write your will:

- A complete list of family information–the names and ages of all members as well as any legal considerations (adoptions, divorces) and the health status for each

- A complete list of all your assets (use the worksheet in Chapter 8)

- A complete list of all your liabilities, or debts (again, use the worksheet in Chapter 8)

- Records of all your insurance policies of any kind (use the information you gathered in Part I)

- An itemized list of all real estate you own, even real estate you own jointly with others (such as your spouse)

- Any inheritances you expect to receive before you die

As you write your will, keep the following in mind:

- All your debts will have to be paid out of your estate before your heirs receive anything. So will your taxes and your burial expenses. The best way to cope with these is to set aside a special fund specifically for payment of debts, taxes, and burial expenses. Your attorney can help you construct the fund and estimate the expenses. (You'll need to review these every two years to allow for inflation.)

- You can disown (*disinherit*) most members of your family, including your children, but you cannot disown your spouse. In most states, your spouse is entitled to at least one-third of your assets, even if you do not specify that in your will.

• You need to be detailed about the disposition of your property. Details guarantee that your wishes will be fulfilled and reduce the risk of costly legal battles for your heirs.

• There are certain things you can't dispose of in your will. You can't dispose of any property that you've already designated a beneficiary for–such as U.S. Savings Bonds, life insurance benefits, and pension funds. You also can't dispose of "exempt" property (it automatically goes to your spouse and children), property you own jointly with someone else, or property you haven't actually received yet (such as an inheritance you are expecting but don't yet have).

• You are legally free to leave part of your estate to a college, church, or charity, but the laws that govern such gifts are tightly regulated and vary from state to state. If you want to make provision in your will for a charitable gift, consult an attorney.

Ready to actually write your will? As mentioned, stationery stores provide forms that guide you through the process. You can start by filling these out; an attorney can then prepare a final copy. Some people leave hand-written wills ("holographic" wills), but these are much more likely to be legally challenged.

Your will should consist of eight simple sections:

1. An opening statement–give your legal name, list your address, and make a statement that you are providing the will by your own free choice.

2. A statement that you are revoking any previous wills or codicils you may have made.

3. Name your executor–the person(s) you are appointing to carry out your wishes and the terms of your will. Most people appoint a spouse, trusted relative, or close friend. The executor should be someone whose judgment you trust, who lives nearby, and who is familiar with your affairs; by law, an executor must be at least twenty-one and a U.S. citizen. *If you don't name at least one executor, the court will appoint one for you–and a court-appointed executor may not have your family's interests as a priority.*

4. Provide a fund for the payment of debts, taxes, and burial expenses, and direct that these be paid promptly.

5. If you have children under the age of twenty-one, specify who those children should live with in case your spouse dies at the same time you do; specify who will be guardian of their property and assets until they reach twenty-one. *If you do not specify a guardian for your children, the state will appoint one–and it may not always be a family member or friend of your family.*

6. Specify how you want your estate distributed. Be specific.

7. If you are leaving part of your estate in trust, specify who the trustees are. As with the executor, the trustee must be twenty-one and a U.S. citizen. You can appoint the same person as executor and trustee, but that's not always advisable.

8. Finally, sign the will, date your signature, and have your witnesses sign and date the will. You should have at least two witnesses. These witnesses each need to attach a statement to your will saying that they saw you sign the will, that you did it of your own free will, and that you asked them to witness.

When you die, the *probate* process begins. Simply stated, the will is brought before the court to establish validity, and creditors are given an opportunity to file claims before the estate is distributed. For more details about probate, see Chapter 18. Depending on the complexity of the will and the estate, probate can be a lengthy, expensive process; even with simple wills, probate generally costs 5 percent of the estate.

Living Trusts

One of the best ways to avoid probate completely is to set up a *living trust*–a trust you create while you are alive. Simply stated, you put all your assets into a "trust," specify that your trust will pay all its income to you as long as you are alive, then specify that the trust will be automatically transferred to your heirs when you die. A *revocable* trust means you reserve the right to change, add to, or revoke the trust as long as you live; this kind of arrangement provides you maximum control over your property and reduces estate taxes.

There are several sound advantages to living trusts:

 • Your estate remains completely private–no one finds out what you had or who inherited it.

- Your heirs avoid legal fees, name changes, and other hassles.

- Your beneficiary can collect your life insurance proceeds and can use them immediately, without the court's approval.

- Your estate is not tied up in probate court, but is immediately available to your heirs–who can generally carry on as usual.

Make sure you contact an attorney and set up any trust with competent legal advice.

Durable Power of Attorney

Finally, consider giving *power of attorney* (the power to act on your behalf) to someone else in case you become unable to make your own decisions. Stationery stores have forms you can fill out, as do some hospitals; consult your attorney for help.

NOTES, CHANGES, AND UPDATES

Chapter 10
The Probate Process

Once first priorities and immediate concerns have been dealt with, you will need to go through the probate process *unless all of your spouse's property was part of a living trust.* (See Chapter 9 for an explanation of living trusts.)

You'll start the process by finding the will. You should know whether a will exists and where it's located; if you're not sure, start by checking through your spouse's papers and any safe deposit boxes. You may also contact your spouse's attorney to determine whether a will had been drawn, signed, and witnessed.

In most states, anyone possessing a will needs to submit it to the probate court within thirty days of the death; failure to do so can bring penalty of law. It is also considered a crime to destroy a will.

Once you've located the will, here's what to expect:

The will is submitted to the probate court. Send the original will to the probate court in the district where your spouse had permanent residency at the time of death. If you cannot find the original, you can submit a certified copy, but you need to be prepared to prove that the will has not been altered. In most cases, the person named as executor needs to petition the court to accept the will.

If your spouse died without leaving a will, you need to petition the probate court to appoint an administrator of the estate; you will also need to submit a list of all the obvious heirs to the court.

Heirs and interested parties are notified. The probate court next orders that all heirs and "interested parties" (such as creditors) be notified that the will has been filed and an executor has been appointed. In some states, such notice must be published in the newspaper. A certain period of time is then allowed for people who object to acceptance of the will or the appointment of the executor.

The executor is appointed. If no one objects, the court officially appoints the executor. Once appointed by the court, the executor takes title to all the deceased person's property, including real estate, securities, bank accounts, and other assets.

The executor files an inventory of the estate. The executor is required by law to file a complete inventory of the estate within a specified period of time–usually within three months of the death. This inventory becomes a matter of public record and is available for public scrutiny; beneficiaries and creditors alike can see what the estate contains.

Claims are paid. By law, claims against the estate must be filed within a specified period of time–usually within six to twelve months. Claims filed after that time do not have to be paid, regardless of whether they are valid. The executor is then responsible for paying the debts, taxes, expenses, and fees associated with the estate.

Estate tax returns are filed. The executor is also responsible for filing estate tax returns; the IRS generally has up to one year to either accept the returns or to request more information. Generally, federal taxes do not have to be paid on estates valued at less than $600,000.

Beneficiaries are paid. *After all claims and taxes are paid*, the executor distributes whatever is left to the beneficiaries of the estate. If a will was left, the executor follows the instructions set out in the will; if no will was left, the executor distributes property according to the laws of the state. Generally, the executor provides each beneficiary with an accounting of what has transpired with the estate; each beneficiary is required to sign a release. *Never sign a release until you are satisfied that the executor's accounting is accurate and appropriate.*

The estate is closed. After all obligations are paid and the remaining estate is distributed to beneficiaries, the executor once again petitions the probate court for settlement and release of the estate. Acceptance of such a petition indicates that the court is satisfied and that the records are considered complete and accurate.

Here Is What Happens To Your Estate At Death!

Personal Property	Real Estate Holdings	Life Ins. & Annuities	Business Holdings

TOTAL ESTATE

DEDUCTIONS
Death Taxes
Income Taxes
CPA Fees
Appraiser Fees

DEDUCTIONS
Probate Fees
Attorney Fees
Court Costs
Executor Fees

THIS IS WHAT IS LEFT FOR HEIRS.

77

NOTES, CHANGES, AND UPDATES

Part III

Planning for the Future

Chapter 11
Disposing of Personal Property

The most difficult and time-consuming part of drafting a will is usually deciding how you're going to dispose of your property.

To get started, follow these guidelines:

• Begin by listing all the people who are important in your life– those you want to receive some of your property. Your spouse, children, and grandchildren are obvious choices, but don't forget good friends, valued business associates, or people who have provided loyal service to you.

• Next, make a list of your property. The worksheet in Chapter 4 can be a good place to start. List *everything*–clothing, jewelry, stamp and coin collections, art objects, furniture, appliances, and anything else that will have to be disposed of in some way.

• Now start matching things up to people. Be specific.

Are there items left over? You have two basic choices:

• You can instruct the executor of your estate to sell the items. Be specific about what you want done; give an approximate price you expect the item to draw.

• You can instruct your executor to donate the items to charity. If you have a favorite charity, make sure you specify it.

You might consider disposing of your property yourself, starting **now**–especially if there are art objects, jewelry, collections, or other things you don't need for day-to-day living. You will have the satisfaction and joy of watching your heirs enjoy their gifts, and you can be guaranteed that your wishes are carried out if you bestow the property yourself.

Chapter 12
Organ Donations and Living Wills

You may want to consider two other things closely related to wills: the wish to donate your vital organs and instruction that your life not be artificially prolonged.

In most states you can legally specify that you want your vital organs donated for transplant or your body made available for medical research. To do it, obtain a donor card, fill it out, sign it, and have a witness sign it. You can obtain a donor card from The Living Bank, P.O. Box 6725, Houston, TX 77265. Most donor cards allow you to specify exactly which organs you want to donate. Many states let you declare your intention to donate on your driver's license.

If you want to become an organ donor, make sure your close family members and physician are aware of your wishes; even though you declare your wishes in a will, organs must be "harvested" immediately and that decision can't be made a week or two later when the will is being read.

You can also draft a *living will*–your instruction that you don't want physicians to prolong your life in the event that you have an incurable injury, disease, or illness certified to be terminal by two physicians. Basically, you express the right to be allowed to die naturally.

Living wills are legal in several states; your attorney can help you draft a will that will be legally recognized in your state. Living wills are generally valid for only five years after they are signed, so make sure you draft a new living will every five years. Make sure you sign the will, date your signature, and have at least two witnesses sign and date the will.

Sample Living Will

Note: *The laws regarding living wills vary from one state to another. The sample living will on the next page is provided **only** **as a sample;** you should consult an attorney to determine the laws in your state before drafting your own living will.*

DIRECTIVE TO PHYSICIANS

DIRECTIVE MADE THIS _____DAY OF ____,____.

I, _____, being of sound mind, willfully and voluntarily make known my desire that my life shall not be artificially prolonged under the circumstances set forth below, do hereby declare:

    1. If at any time I should have an incurable injury, disease, or illness certified to be a terminal condition by two physicians, and where the application of life-sustaining procedures would serve only to artificially prolong the moment of my death and where my physician determines that my death is imminent whether or not life-sustaining procedures are utilized, I direct that such procedures be withheld or withdrawn, and that I be permitted to die naturally.

    2. In the absence of my ability to give directions regarding the use of such life-sustaining procedures, it is my intention that this directive shall be honored by my family and physicians as the final expression of my legal right to refuse medical or surgical treatment and accept the consequences from such refusal.

    3. If I have been diagnosed as pregnant and that diagnosis is known to my physician, this directive shall have no force or effect during the course of my pregnancy.

    4. I have been diagnosed and notified at least 14 days ago as having a terminal condition by _____, M.D. I understand that if I have not filled in the physician's name, it shall be presumed that I did not have a terminal condition when I made out this directive.

    5. This directive shall have no force or effect after five years from the date filled in above.

    6. I understand the full impact of this directive and I am emotionally and mentally competent to make this directive.

[The will must be signed and witnessed according to law]

NOTES, CHANGES, AND UPDATES

Chapter 13
Funeral Arrangements

If you thought funeral arrangements are something done only by grieving survivors, think again: **you can make your own funeral arrangements while you are alive and healthy**.

Sound strange? It's not! Just as you want to specify what happens to your property and possessions when you die, you also have the right to specify what happens to your body–where you're buried and what kind of funeral services you have–when you die. *This kind of planning is especially important if you have already purchased a cemetery plot, if you have prepaid your funeral expenses through an insurance policy, or you have strong wishes about the type of funeral service.*

Take some time to think about what you want; if you're married, you will probably want to discuss your wishes with your spouse. Then fill out the following worksheet and make your spouse and other family members aware it.

Obituary/Death Notice

• You want an obituary/death notice in the following newspapers

_____

_____

Note: Don't forget alumni magazines or newspapers and professional publications.
• You do not want death notices to appear.

Disposition of the Body

• You want to be buried
• You want to be cremated
> • You want your remains to be buried
> • You want your remains to be scattered if permitted by law at _____
• You want to be entombed
• You want your body to be donated to_____

Viewing of the Body

• You prefer that mourners not be able to view your body before the service.
• You have no objection to mourners viewing your body before the service.

Type of Casket

You want the following kind of casket:
> • Metal
> • Hardwood
> • Softwood covered with cloth

You want the casket:
> • Closed at all times
> • Open only for close family and friends
> • Open for anyone attending the service
>> • Before the service
>> • During the service

Flowers

You want flowers to be sent:
- By anyone who wishes to send them
- By close family and friends only
- Not at all

After the services, you would like the following to be done with the flowers:
- Placed on your grave
- Distributed among your survivors
- Taken to the following local hospital, rest home, or other:_

_____

Instead of flowers, you would prefer gifts or donations to the following:_____

_____

Type of Service

You want the following type of service:
- A service with your body present, but only close family and friends invited to attend
- A service with your body present and anyone welcome
- A memorial service without your body present, with only close family and friends invited to attend
- A memorial service without your body present and anyone welcome to attend

You want the following eight people to serve as pallbearers:

1._____
2._____
3._____
4._____
5._____
6._____
7._____
8._____

You would like the following included in your service:

Prayers_____
Scriptures_____
Readings_____
Music_____
Other_____

Burial or Entombment

You want to be buried at_____
You want the following kind of burial marker:

> • Metal flush with the ground
> • Stone flush with the ground
> • Stone upright
>
> *Note: Some cemeteries have restrictions; you should check with the one where you would like to be buried or entombed about possible size and style restrictions.*

You would like the following engraved on your marker:

_____

_____

Part IV

Medicare and Social Security

NOTES, CHANGES, AND UPDATES

Chapter 14
Social Security

Depending on your age, your coverage, and your spouse's coverage, you can be eligible for Social Security benefits as early as age sixty.

What Is Social Security?

All Americans who work pay payroll taxes–among them Social Security taxes. Receipts from those taxes are then paid directly into the U.S. Treasury and credited to a trust fund. Retirees and others who qualify for Social Security are paid from the U.S. Treasury.

The government tightly controls Social Security funds. Taxes collected for Social Security can be used only to pay benefits and administrative costs. Less than 1 percent of the total amount collected in the last sixty years has been used for administrative costs.

Beginning in 1983, Social Security taxes were increased so that the system could build up enough reserves to take care of future generations who would need Social Security. Officials estimate that taxes will take care of expenditures until about the year 2013; interest will pay benefits for an additional six years; and the accumulated reserves will pay benefits through the year 2030. Congress is currently considering several ways to correct long-term deficits.

It's very possible that future generations will face increased Social Security taxes if the system is to stay solvent.

General Eligibility

At age sixty, you are probably eligible for survivor benefits *if*:
- Your spouse is deceased, *and*
- Your spouse was covered under the Social Security program

Never cash a Social Security check made payable to your deceased spouse. Instead, return it to the Social Security Administration, which will issue you a check in your own name.

At age sixty-two, if you are covered by the Social Security program, you can elect early retirement and receive Social Security benefits. If you're still working and your income exceeds the allowable amount, you may want to defer retirement.

If you are not yet seventy and your personal earned income is more than the limit set by the Social Security Administration, you could lose part or all of your Social Security benefits. If your spouse is also receiving benefits on your earnings, your spouse will also lose those benefits.

At age seventy, you may earn any amount and still draw Social Security benefits.

How to Apply

Remember: **Social Security benefits are not automatic.** *You must apply for them.* Call your local office of the Social Security Administration to find out how to apply, how much you are eligible for, and what qualifications you must meet.

Plan on applying for Social Security benefits about three months before you are eligible to receive the actual benefits.

Social Security laws change frequently, and the amount you are eligible for may change from one year to the next. A free hand-book available from the Social Security Administration explains these changes and details up-to-date information about benefits and eligibility.

NOTES, CHANGES, AND UPDATES

Chapter 15
Medicare

In essence, Medicare is a federally funded medical insurance program that covers Americans in certain categories. To qualify for Medicare, you must meet one of the following conditions:

- You are at least sixty-five years old, and you or your spouse have paid into the Social Security system for at least ten years
- You are at least sixty-five years old and "buy" into the system without having paid into the Social Security system for at least ten years
- You qualify for Railroad Retirement
- You qualify for Social Security Disability and have met the two-year waiting period
- You have end-stage kidney disease

What Medicare Covers

There are two parts to Medicare: Part A, which is automatic for most Americans, and Part B, for which individuals pay premiums.

Part A
Most people automatically receive a Medicare card when they turn sixty-five; that means you're already enrolled in Part B. Under Part A, you pay a small deductible, and Medicare pays for all inpatient hospital care during the first sixty days of each illness. Medicare pays a smaller percentage of fees for an additional thirty days of inpatient hospital care. After that, your supplemental insurance needs to take over.

Part A also covers care in a skilled nursing facility and some home-health care, post-hospital care, and hospice care.

Most people do not pay any premium for Part A.

Part B
You need to *apply* for Part B, which is optional. You must apply for it during the three months before you turn sixty-five, or during the first three months of each following year (called an "open enrollment" period). Once you have coverage, you need to pay a monthly premium. Premiums are generally higher if you enroll during one of these open enrollment periods instead of the period before you turn sixty-five.

Under Part B, you pay an annual deductible for medical and outpatient services. After that, Medicare pays 80 percent of all physician and outpatient care, home-health care, and other medical services. You must pay the remaining 20 percent–either out of your pocket or through supplemental health insurance. Depending on your physician's policies, he or she may bill Medicare directly for the 80 percent, and bill you only for the remaining 20 percent.

Medicare does *not* cover:

- Prescription drugs for anyone other than hospitalized patients
- Hearing aids
- Eyeglasses
- Preventive services
- Medical care received outside the United States

How to Apply

You can receive Medicare benefits at age sixty-five *even if* you decide not to apply for Social Security benefits then.

You'll probably automatically get a Medicare card in the mail when you turn sixty-five. You'll also automatically get a Medicare card if you apply for Social Security or Railroad Retirement at any age.

You'll need to apply for Part B if you decide you want that coverage. You should apply during the three months before you turn sixty-five at your local Social Security Administration office.

Questions?

A free Medicare handbook is available from the Social Security Administration. It gives up-to-date information on deductibles, premiums, eligibility, coverage, and benefits, which can change frequently.

The Medicare handbook also details the process through which you can appeal decisions on payments.

Counseling offices are located in each state to answer questions about Medicare coverage. To find the office in your state, call the Medicare hotline, toll-free, at 1-800-638-6833.

NOTES, CHANGES, AND UPDATES

Part V

Priorities

Chapter 16
When Death Is Imminent

Few things are more painful or difficult to face than the impending death of someone you love. But being willing to face that eventuality can give you a sense of security and can bless your loved one with peace of mind.

You can make sure your loved one's wishes are carried out **by acting now**. Follow these guidelines:

• If the person is coherent, fill in as many areas of this handbook as you can. The information you gather will make things much easier after the death.

• Review the will with the person and make sure all items, instructions, and wishes are current. If they are not, help the person make a codicil. Be sure to involve an attorney and witnesses.

• If necessary, obtain a power of attorney.

• If you haven't already talked about it, plan the funeral arrangements; you can follow the outline in Chapter 12. Assure your loved one that you are trying to make sure his/her wishes are carried out regarding the type of casket, type of ceremony, and so on.

• You may want to set up a standby trust that would allow the easy transfer of property upon death but that would end if the crisis passes and the person recovers. Talk to an attorney if you have questions.

• Contact members of your professional help team to find out what else you should do. The worksheet in Chapter 16 will help you gather the names, numbers, and addresses of those who can help now and after death occurs.

Chapter 17
First Priorities

When someone you love dies, you need to take immediate action. That might seem difficult or impossible; you can feel riveted to the spot, frozen in time. You're likely to feel that your life will never be the same again. It probably won't. But, with good planning and preparation, you can accomplish the tasks that need to be done quickly and without difficulty.

The following priorities **must be dealt with as soon as possible after death occurs:**

Arrange for removal of the body. A hospital or nursing home will usually hold the body for several hours while you decide what you want done. Funeral homes or crematoriums will pick up the body for you. If the body is to be donated, you need to immediately contact the medical school, organ bank, or other facility.

If you are still undecided or need to contact other family members before you can commit to a funeral home, call any local funeral home and ask that they simply remove and hold the body. *Make sure to specify that you only want the home to hold the body until you make further arrangements or decisions.*

Arrange for child care. If you have small children, arrange for their care immediately. Ideally, they should be cared for by someone they know and trust; discuss the death with sensitivity and regard to their age. You may need help from your clergyman or a counselor.

Notify family and friends. You should probably be the one to contact close family members; consider asking someone else to contact others for you. Remember to contact the person's employer.

Meet with the clergy. Call your clergyman both for notification and for help in planning the funeral service, dealing with small children, or other concerns.

Contact the funeral home. In most cases, you can call the funeral home immediately, and they will pick up the body and transport it for you. Normally you need to go to the funeral home within a day and meet with the funeral director to plan for services and burial. Keep the following in mind:

• Arrange to take someone with you to the funeral home.
• Write down ahead of time what you want to appear in the death notice or obituary. Take along a list of newspapers and publications where you want the death notice to appear.
• Have a good idea ahead of time about what you want for the funeral service, casket, and burial; you'll be less prone to overspend or forget important details.
• The funeral director's job is to comfort and help you, but you *pay* for those services. Keep in mind that you don't have to use **all** the services the funeral director offers–ask for only what you need, and pay for only what you use.
• Early in your discussion with the funeral director, make your wishes known. This helps focus the discussion and eliminates unnecessary choices.
• Don't be embarrassed about asking for pricing information; you need it to make wise decisions, and you are going to have to pay for the funeral. Request price information in writing.
• If your funeral home offers a "package" deal, look it over carefully. Many of these deals include things you would not normally use. You may be better off ordering–and paying for–only the individual things you will need.
• One of the biggest expenses will be the casket. Remember: it's a piece of merchandise, and it's in the funeral director's best interest

to sell you an expensive one. Decide before you get to the funeral home how much you want to spend on a casket; your preplanning will help you resist a skillful sales pitch. If you are not shown a casket in the price range or style you want, ask for it.

• Remember that you don't need to have the funeral at the funeral home, even if you use the home's services. You might have the funeral in a church or at a private home instead.

Decide on pallbearers. You'll need to specify six to eight men as pallbearers. The spouse is generally not asked to serve as a pallbearer, but you might consider children, grandchildren, other close relatives, and close friends. You can given the designation of *honorary pallbearer* to someone too elderly or infirm to actually participate in carrying the casket.

Make cemetery arrangements. If the person does not already own cemetery space, you'll need to purchase it now. You'll also need to make arrangements with the cemetery for burial. If there is more than one cemetery in your area, don't be afraid to compare! Check out the following:

- Price differences
- Regulations, such as what kind of grave markers are allowed and what kind of grave liners are required
- Whether perpetual care is provided
- The cemetery's reputation

Contact the members of your professional help team. You'll list them on the worksheet in Chapter 16. Arrange for various services you need from your attorney, accountant, banker, or insurance agent.

Check the safe deposit box. If you have a safe deposit box, check its contents as soon as you can; many banks now allow anyone listed on the box to have free access, even if one person has died. Remove the will immediately; you'll need it when you meet with your attorney. You might also want to remove other things now–it may be awhile before you get back around to it.

Pay necessary bills. Some bills will be due immediately; take care of those. *A note of caution:* bills will probably arrive months after the death that you know nothing about. **Do not pay any bill unless you are certain it is valid.** If you question the bill, call the creditor, request appropriate copies, and ask for verification. If you need further help, contact your attorney or accountant. If you are unfamiliar with banking practices or how to use a checkbook, meet with your banker for help.

Take care of miscellaneous chores. You may need to consider the following:

• If you didn't live with the deceased, you need to arrange for care of the person's home and property. You might arrange for some-one to stay at the house; burglars often read obituaries and prey on homes they think will be unguarded.

• Use a notebook to keep track of gifts, flowers, and other expressions of sympathy. You'll want to send thank-you notes or other acknowledgements later, and it's too difficult to rely on memory regarding people who sent flowers, brought in meals, shoveled your walks, or did other services.

• If guests are coming from out of town, make arrangements for their lodging. While it's always nicer to stay in someone's home, resist the stress and pressure of feeling that *you* have to accommodate out-of-town guests. It might be easier and less stressful for everyone if you can make arrangements for a nice hotel.

• As flowers and plants begin to arrive, some will be sent to the funeral home or church, but many will be sent to your home. Consider what you might want to do with them. Shut-ins in your neighborhood, people in hospitals, or patients at nursing homes can derive a great deal of pleasure from beautiful sprays, wreaths, and arrangements after the funeral.

NOTES, CHANGES, AND UPDATES

Chapter 18
Contacts You Need to Make

Depending on your circumstances, you may need to make the following contacts:

Military organizations. If you or your spouse were ever in the military, your funeral director can help you prepare forms for the Veterans Administration. Have the life insurance policy number, the branch of service, the serial number, and discharge papers available when you fill out the forms. If you have children between the ages of eighteen and twenty-five, they may qualify for benefits under the War Orphans and Widows Assistance Act.

Fraternal and service clubs. If either spouse belongs to a fraternal organization or service club (such as the Elks, Shrines, Kiwanis, or Rotary), check with representatives about available benefits or services. Many of these organizations help with funeral arrangements and can provide pallbearers.

Civil Service. If the deceased died in service after eighteen months on the job, was married for two years, and had children or was disabled, you are eligible for benefits. You can file forms at any federal agency or Civil Service bureau; see the sample letter in Chapter 17.

Social Security. You are eligible for benefits if your spouse was a covered worker over the age of sixty; you are eligible for additional benefits if you have minor children. If you are also covered under Social Security, check with them on possible changes in your current benefits. Remember: **Social Security benefits are not automatic; you must apply for them.** If you receive a check payable to the deceased, *do not cash it*; return it to the Social

Security administration.

Medicare. If your spouse was hospitalized prior to death, make sure you get full Medicare coverage if eligible. While Medicare pays part of hospital and drug expenses, it does not pay 100 percent; you will need to pay the remainder or file with another insurance company for coverage. Be aware that the following items *are not paid by Medicare*:

- Private nurses
- Eye exams and glasses
- Services covered by Workmans Compensation
- Normal dental work and dentures
- Personal comfort items
- The first three pints of transfused blood
- Routine foot care
- Hearing aids
- Custodial care

This list of exclusions will likely change under Clinton's health reform package. Call your local office for an update on coverage and the benefits you are entitled to.

Life insurance. Contact insurance agents for each policy; have the policy number on hand before you call. You'll need a certified copy of the death certificate in order to collect on the policy. Most life insurance companies will let you leave the funds on deposit, earning interest, until you decide what you want to do with the money. Remember: **you do not need an attorney to help you collect on a life insurance policy.** (If your spouse was listed as one of *your* beneficiaries, you should change that on your policy now.)

Employer. Even if your spouse was self-employed, there may be benefits available through employment; make sure you also check with all previous employers. Ask specifically about life insurance benefits, disability benefits, 401K investment plans, and retirement plans. You should also find out whether it's possible for you to convert or continue your spouse's health and disability insurance.

Social organizations. Social organizations, unions, auto clubs, and professional organizations may provide some benefits. You may also want to consider selling memberships in social clubs (such as country clubs or tennis clubs) to raise funds; postpone making that kind of decision for at least six months, and check into your rights before you finalize your plans.

Older Americans Act. A variety of community services are funded by the Older Americans Act through local Area Agencies on Aging. You can get information, emergency numbers, transportation, homemaking, medical equipment, nutrition and meal delivery, adult day care services, counseling, support groups, social and recreational activities, and maintenance services (such as laundry, shopping, and errands). *Where to Turn for Help for Older Persons* is available from the Superintendent of Documents, U.S. Government Printing Office, Washington, DC 20402.

Banks and Savings and Loans. Try to locate all bank accounts; in some states, accounts that are inactive for five years are turned over to the state. The IRS may be able to help you locate bank accounts, since banks report any earned interest over $10 from any account.

Utility services. You may want to change the name on your utility accounts. You should also ask utility representatives to help you locate the main gas and water shut-offs, electrical fuses, and circuit breakers; learn how to open the garage door if the automatic door opener is not working; how to have the fire extinguisher serviced; and other things you are unclear about.

NOTES, CHANGES, AND UPDATES

Chapter 19
Your Professional Help Team

Attorney

Name_____

Firm_____

Address_____

City_____ State_____ Zip_____

Phone_____

Accountant

Name_____

Firm_____

Address_____

City_____ State_____ Zip_____

Phone_____

Insurance agents (life, health, general)

Name_____

Firm_____

Address_____

City_____ State_____ Zip_____

Phone_____

Name_____

Firm_____

Address_____

City_____ State_____ Zip_____

Phone_____

NOTES, CHANGES, AND UPDATES

Insurance agents (life, health, general, *continued*)
Name_____

Firm_____

Address_____

City_____ State_____ Zip_____

Phone_____

Financial planner
Name_____

Firm_____

Address_____

City_____ State_____ Zip_____

Phone_____

Investment broker
Name_____

Firm_____

Address_____

City_____ State_____ Zip_____

Phone_____

Banker
Name_____

Firm_____

Address_____

City_____ State_____ Zip_____

Phone_____

Trust officer
Name_____

Firm_____

Address_____

City_____ State_____ Zip_____

Phone_____

NOTES, CHANGES, AND UPDATES

Chapter 20
Sample Letters

In writing business letters, you should keep all lines flush against the left margin; do not indent paragraphs. Letters should be typewritten if possible, single-spaced, on one side of a white sheet of paper. Begin each letter with the date, followed by two spaces, then the name and full address of the recipient.

The following are sample letters you can copy in your correspondence with life insurance companies, the Social Security Administration, and the Civil Service.

To a life insurance company:

[Date]

[Name of agent]
[Company]
[Address]
[City, state, zip]

Ref: [The insured's name and policy number]

To Whom It May Concern:

This is to advise you that my [husband/wife] passed away on
[month, day, year] at [location]. The cause of death was [as listed
on the death certificate]. Please send me the correct forms for
filing a claim on [his/her] insurance policy. As beneficiary, I
would like all information on every settlement option. Please
search your files for any other policies the insured may have had.

Sincerely,

[Your name]
[Address]
[City, state, zip]
[Phone]

To the Social Security Administration:

[Date]

[Local office]
[Address]
[City, state, zip]

Ref: [Name and Social Security number]

To Whom It May Concern:

My [husband/wife] died on [month, day, year] at [location]. As the named beneficiary, I would like to schedule an appointment to discuss possible benefits. Please let me know what documents you will need in addition to the death certificate.

Sincerely,

[Your name]
[Address]
[City, state, zip]
[Phone]
[Your Social Security number]

Note: You may want to call the local Social Security information office first; agents there can help you with immediate concerns.

To the Civil Service Commission:

[Date]

Civil Service Commission
1900 E Street, N.W.
Washington, D.C. 20415

Ref: [Deceased's name]

To Whom It May Concern:

My [husband/wife] died on [month, day, year] at [location]. As the named beneficiary, I need the forms necessary to file a claim. Please let me know what documents will be needed in addition to the death certificate.

Sincerely,

[Your name]
[Address]
[City, state, zip]
[Phone]
[Your Social Security number]

Depending on your circumstances, you may also need to send letters requesting information on benefits to the following:

Railroad Retirement
844 Rush Street
Chicago, IL 60611

Social Security
6400 Security Boulevard
Baltimore, MD 21335

U.S. Department of Health and Human Services
Social Security Administration
Western Program Service Center
P.O. Box 2072
Richmond, CA 94802

Veterans Administration
Eastern U.S.A.
500 Wissahickon Avenue
Philadelphia, PA 19010

Veterans Administration
Western U.S.A.
Fort Snelling
St. Paul, MN 55111

Check your local phone directory for the addresses of fraternal and service organizations.

NOTES, CHANGES, AND UPDATES

Appendices

Appendix A
Service and Utility List

Use the following sample name change list to change ownership or billing services for utilities–not only in the event of a death, but if you move. **List names and phone numbers.**

Mortgage company (1st) _____

Mortgage company (2nd) _____

Tax collector _____

Insurance agents _____

_____

Burglar alarm company _____

Gas company _____

Telephone company _____

City utilities _____

County utilities _____

Pest control _____

Cable television _____

Pool service _____

Garage door company _____

Gardener _____

Newspapers _____

_____

Credit card companies _____

_____

_____

Social clubs _____

_____

_____

Gym or spa _____

Motor vehicle dept. _____

Auto insurance company _____

Banks _____

_____

_____

_____

Investment companies _____

_____

_____

Credit unions _____

_____

_____

Others _____

_____

_____

_____

_____

Appendix B
Document Location List

Item	Location
Adoption papers	_____
Annuity policies	_____
Agreements	_____
Bank books	_____
Bank statements	_____
Birth certificates	_____
Cash	_____
Cemetery plot/crypt	_____
Citizenship papers	_____
Church membership	_____
Club memberships	_____
Copyrights	_____
Deeds	_____
Divorce papers	_____
Driver's licenses	_____
Durable power atty.	_____
Expenses paid	_____
Family trust	_____
Funeral arrg.	_____
Home inventory	_____
Income statements	_____
Income tax records	_____
IRA accounts	_____
Insurance	_____
Investments	_____
Keogh account	_____
Leases	_____
Living will	_____

Marriage certificate _____

Military records _____

Mortgages _____

Notes receivable _____

Notes payable _____

Paid bills _____

Passports _____

Patents _____

Pension plans _____

Pet records _____

Receipts _____

Rental agreements _____

Safe deposit box _____

Securities _____

Social Security card _____

Trademarks _____

Trusts _____

Vehicle titles _____

Vehicle finances _____

Warranties _____

Wills _____

Appendix C
Glossary

Annuity Return of investment now or in the future.

Assets Items that can usually be converted into money.

Broker One who buys or sells for another for a commission.

C.D. A Certificate of Deposit from a bank or savings and loan.

C.L.U. Chartered Life Underwriter (a professional designation in the life insurance industry).

C.P.A. Certified Public Accountant.

Codicil A supplement or addition to a will.

Deferred comp Compensation deferred by an employer until a later date.

Defined benefit A type of retirement plan that allows the amount normally paid at retirement to be paid in advance.

Family revocable living trust A living trust created while you are alive that enables your assets to be kept out of probate when you die.

F.I.C.A. The Federal Insurance Compensation Act (more commonly known as Social Security).

H.M.O. Health Maintenance Organization.

I.R.A. Individual Retirement Plan, normally allowing tax-deferred contributions of a certain percentage of income.

IRS Internal Revenue Service.

KEOGH A retirement plan for those who are self-employed.

Liabilities Debts or obligations.

Limited partnership An investment where you as a limited partner are not liable for the acts of general partners.

Joint venture A special type of partnership.

K1 An income tax reporting form sent to investors.

Living will A form expressing your desire **not** to use artificial methods to extend your life.

Money purchase A type of retirement plan where money is deposited to buy a deferred annuity.

Mortgage A conditional transfer of property pledged as security for the repayment of a loan.

Net worth Total assets minus total liabilities.

Probate A process used by the court to check the validity of a will.

Profit-sharing plan An employer retirement plan in which employees receive a percentage of the profits of the company.

S&L Savings and loan.

Trust Custody and care of assets.

VA Veterans Administration.

Will The legal document of giving or bequeathing.

W2 Employee income reporting form.

401K Employer/employee tax-deferred investment plan.

1098 Form given by the mortgage lender on the interest paid.

1099 Form given by employers to report income.

NOTES, CHANGES, AND UPDATES

NOTES, CHANGES, AND UPDATES

NOTES, CHANGES, AND UPDATES